THE SIX SIGMA METHOD

Boost quality and consistency
in your business

Written by Anis Ben Alaya
In collaboration with Amicie de Quatrebarbes
Translated by Carly Probert

Business 50MINUTES.com

THE SIX SIGMA METHOD

KEY INFORMATION

- **Names:** Six Sigma, 6 Sigma, 6 σ
- **Uses:** a qualitative, quantitative and structured approach to business management.
- **Why is it successful?** It is a precise approach to improve key business processes for a reliability of more than 99.99%. The objective is to achieve an average of 3.4 defects per one million defect opportunities (where 3.8 sigma, for example, corresponds to 10 000 defects per million).
- **Key words:**
  - Customers: all agents interested in a product or service
  - Defect: product imperfection
  - DMAIC: managerial method with the objective of improving a product or service
  - Information: data used to establish a comprehensive view of a given situation, without leaving out details
  - Performance: numerical result
  - Process: different stages of production
  - Project management: approach used within a company for organising a project in different stages
  - Quality: defining characteristics of a product
  - Sigma (σ): Greek letter representing standard deviation in statistics
  - Standard deviation: variation or dispersion of a variable against a threshold (the average)
  - Statistical tool: analysis method for a database, following a numerical approach

- Strategic objective: aimed balance, involving actions that lead to the benefit of a favourable market position

INTRODUCTION

Faced with a product offering that does not satisfy customers or the business enough or at all, the latter may decide to reconsider its workflow (manufacturing, etc.) in order to concretely improve its quality. The Six Sigma method allows you to calibrate new objectives and reduce the probability of variation within a process, once a detailed analysis has been conducted to identify the defects that alter the satisfaction of both the customers and employees, but also the company.

History

In the mid-1980s, the US company Motorola faced considerable pressure from Asian producers, especially the Japanese, because its production system, fundamentally different from the Asian systems, no longer seemed suitable for the realities of the market. Throughout the 1970s, Japanese factories had been more focused on durability and reliability and therefore offered simpler models than those from US factories that put more emphasis on quality elements (model design, options, etc.). US factories then looked to inspections in order to control the products (an unreliable and expensive method).

Faced with a decrease in profits, Motorola executives then chose to change their philosophy and combine statistical tools with leadership principles to form the basis of a comprehensive management system: Six Sigma. The results were immediately visible, as the quality of the products improved instantly. The process started to spread in the 1990s and was adopted by General Electric, which quickly experienced the benefits of this management method.

Today, most major companies have opted for this system: Caterpillar, Kodak, SFR, etc. Six Sigma has become a quality standard in terms of business practice and is taught in many business schools worldwide.

GOOD TO KNOW

Here are some examples of the benefits of Six Sigma:

- Motorola capitalised $2.2 billion between 1986 and 1990;
- General Electric recorded a performance oscillating between $7 and $10 billion in 1995 thanks to this method;
- The Bank of America saved hundreds of millions of dollars, halved its running time and greatly reduced its margins of error, three years after having adopted the method in 2001.

Definition of the model

Six Sigma is an analytical approach based on statistically verified facts which aims to improve the functioning of a company (production, administration, etc., at a lower cost) and to ensure the quality (reliability of 99.99%) of products or services for customers. This method takes its name from a specific statistical tool: standard deviation, represented by the Greek letter σ. In fact, Six Sigma uses process analysis to provide a product in a 'quality gap' (i.e. not more than 3 σ away from the average) expected by the customer and the company. This allows the company to limit the variation and defects in the process.

THEORY

Companies using this quality management method for improving their products focus on three priorities: customers, employees and processes. Prioritising the customers means you can identify them, know their expectations and anticipate the added value the company could provide for them. This seems obvious, yet many companies tend to forget that profit comes from customer satisfaction. The other two priorities must also be at the heart of the company's concerns, because neglecting them could indirectly cause discontent among customers – these three areas are interconnected.

The main priority areas

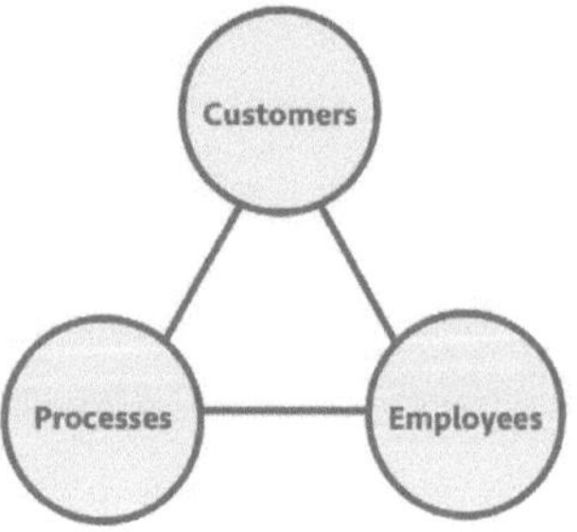

Six Sigma follows two methodologies. Their use depends on the context in which the company wants to expand its production: by extension or creation of a product.

DMAIC

When implementing Six Sigma to improve the results of an existing product or service, you must adhere to the following process, called 'DMAIC':

- **Define**. Defining customers, expectations, team charter with specific measures for organising the project development stage, the general process and financial results.
- **Measure**. Measure and collect data (defects) of the process.
- **Analyse**. Analyse the data collected and the process in order to identify problems related to the current situation.
- **Improve**. Innovate to identify potential solutions, then apply them on a small scale to see if they effectively improve process performance.
- **Control**. Controlling, detailing and implementing a plan to ensure that improvement takes place on a larger scale.

DMADV

The DMAIC methodology is used to improve an existing product or service. Another methodology is used in the case of developing and designing a new product or service: 'DMADV' (Define, Measure, Analyse, Design and Verify).

The Design stage in DMADV involves making the product or establishing the service. The team ensures product compliance.

WHAT IS SIX SIGMA?

On a technical level, Six Sigma is based on the theory of variability, which means that everything is statistically measurable when compared to a continuous scale (weight, height, rate, etc.) that follows a bell-shaped curve. This, called a 'Gaussian curve', is symmetrical and represents virtually 100% of what is measured. It can be divided into several segments – standard deviations marked with the Greek letter σ (sigma) – that define the variability, while the axis represented by the letter μ (mu) is the average that every process approaches. The weaker this variation, the more production is consistent with values close to the target.

Segmented bell curve

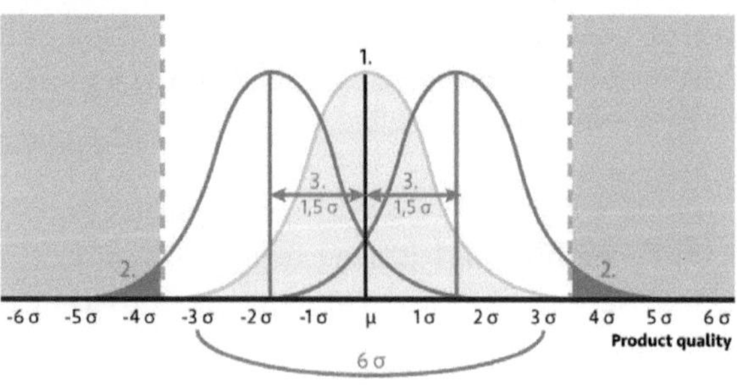

The application of Six Sigma involves measuring the current performance and, to do this, it is necessary to determine the sigma between the real average and the μ average, which shows the perfection of the product or service and thus indirectly shows the average customer satisfaction. Considering customer dissatisfaction as a defect, indicated by a distance from the optimal level of satisfaction, Six Sigma means there will only be 3.4 defects per one million opportunities. In this context, the company focuses on the quality that satisfies the customer to achieve near-perfection: the top of the μ curve. Statistically, the variance cannot be negative. The negative and positive sigma merely express the distance between the product with the maximum average quality that satisfies the customer.

Six Sigma (through good process management) can therefore be used to determine how close the company is to the best performance levels.

However, Six Sigma should not be considered a technical tool. Companies that choose to apply this method must view it as an opportunity that enables them to understand everything that needs to be done to achieve near-perfection and constantly improve performance.

Of course, once a company starts to measure its sigma, it can quickly become discouraged, especially if it notices that many performances are situated in an interval deriving from the optimum (in a level with an absolute value of 1 or 2 σ). But it is necessary to think of this method as a 'permanent dissatisfaction policy' regarding the acquired results. In fact, it encourages all employees to constantly reduce the variations.

PROJECT PLAYERS

Beyond the procedures outlined above, we must not over-look the contribution of other tools used during the various stages of implementing Six Sigma (brainstorming, diagrams, etc.) for constant improvement and continuation of the process. Specifically, various players in society participate in discussions and work on elaborating the upstream method.

Firstly, **the head of the company** must be involved in one way or another in adopting the Six Sigma philosophy and spreading it throughout the organisation, right from the beginning. The team responsible for implementing the improvement process cannot succeed without their full support. People who work on Six Sigma projects are usually part of the most competent areas of the organisation. The hierarchy is made up as follows:

- **Champions** are the guarantors of the project. They help the Black Belts to select improvement projects to work on, estimate their potential and assess the company's products compared to those of the competition. The role of Champions is to ensure the supervision, support and financing of Six Sigma projects and manage the staff needed to implement them. They are the pillars of the project and that is why they are chosen from the best people.
- **Black Belts** are the project leaders and the only people to work full time on it. It is not uncommon for them

to receive prior training in order to better define their mission and directly apply the five phases of the DMAIC methodology leading to Six Sigma.

* **Green Belts** assist the Black Belts in completing the project. They also receive training to enable the team to speak the same language and therefore work towards a common goal.

Six Sigma is the first management method that involves the top of the pyramid as much as the bottom. It is a process that brings a certain dynamic to the business.

LIMITATIONS AND EXTENSIONS

LIMITATIONS AND CRITICISMS

Six Sigma is often seen as a revolutionary and powerful management tool thanks to the performances recorded by the many companies that have adopted it. However, like all methods, it does have some limits, both methodologically and terminologically. Furthermore, as is the case for many other economic aspects, there is a difference between the theoretical and practical aspects. American economist George Eckes, Six Sigma specialist, highlights the failures often observed during applications of the method and offers some recommendations:

- **Consider that quality improvement does not result only from improving statistics.** Rigour and discipline can be significant assets, but they do not cover all the means necessary for the proper management and improvement of a process. Six Sigma combines a series of complementary areas and does not neglect the human aspect in any case, which is both an actor (employees within the company) and a target (customers to satisfy). This aspect is often overlooked during applications within a business.is
- **Realise that reducing costs is only one step of the improvement process.** Six Sigma does not consist of programming cost reductions for strategic purposes. On the contrary, this method advocates efficiency and effectiveness by refocusing the company objectives on customer expectations, rather than an accounting

approach that calculates the known costs and neglects the impact on the customer.

- **Be sure to include improvement in job descriptions.** It is not always easy to reform a process in a company in order to apply Six Sigma. Employees or workers often feel they don't have time for such a re-assessment and believe that they already devote sufficient time to the company. Yet this 'surplus' of time they spend on working for the company is often due to ineffectiveness and inefficiency. This does not necessarily come from the unwillingness of the worker, but rather the process itself.

- **Remember that team dynamic is a leading cause of project failure.** Although it seems easy to manage team dynamics, this is one of the main sources of failure. It is therefore important to build a solid foundation. To do this, the project manager must clearly explain the ins and outs of the project. Meeting supervision, setting the agenda and determining the respective roles and responsibilities are starting points to ensure that the project does not begin on shaky ground.

- **Consider that the Black Belts are not completely responsible for the efforts.** Black Belts are intended to be team leaders. As explained above, they are usually people trained in the use of tools and techniques for improvement – almost like operational leaders. The danger lies in the fact that everyone (including the leaders of the company) separates themselves from the responsibilities of the project as they imagine that domestic experts are there to launch Six Sigma. However, the proper functioning of a company comes from teamwork, and all hierarchical management positions are involved.

- **Consider Six Sigma to be an improvement in continuity.** One of the principles of the method is to work in continuity and constantly ensure a quality process, not to form a team in charge of Six Sigma as soon as an inefficiency or ineffectiveness problem arises in the company.
- **Think of management as an active player.** For Six Sigma to work, the leaders of the company must get their hands dirty and consider themselves participants in the work of the company. Senior management is aware that cultural phenomenon is an important element in business management. One of Six Sigma's strengths is that it encourages a proactive attitude at all hierarchical levels.
- **Be aware of the changes in business management.** If changes at strategic levels are not well managed by the company, the potential results will remain low.

RELATED MODELS AND EXTENSIONS

Lean Six Sigma (LSS)

Lean Six Sigma (LSS) is an extension of Six Sigma that is becoming increasingly important. It is more focused on the production process, while Six Sigma focuses mainly on the product itself. This related model allows you to reduce the working time and waiting periods required for the establishment of a more effective process.

The strategic objectives of this model are:

- increasing the added value of process tasks;
- reducing the time and cost of the process by eliminating activities with no added value;

- making processes more fluid;
- improving the quality of products according to customers;
- encouraging the development of a culture of continuous improvement within the company.

-

- The main areas of action are:
- defining value and identifying the steps that create it;
- identification and elimination of waste and hidden costs;
- control of variation sources by following the steps of the process.

Total Quality Management (TQM)

Total Quality Management is an older quality management approach than Six Sigma. Their common objective is to mobilise the whole company to achieve perfect quality while reducing waste and improving the final product through performance. TQM focuses on the customer – satisfaction and loyalty – although the practice of quality control and self-control is essential here.

The methodology of the model is as follows:

- **Plan.** Development of strategic objectives and schedule improvement plans.
- **Do.** Implementation and application of improved production processes.
- **Check.** Satisfaction analysis and quality control of the product.
- **Act.** Correction of costs and waste and control of production stages.

According to US project management Frank Anbari, Six Sigma is more complete and comprehensive than TQM because it provides financial results and combines advanced analysis tools and managerial methods. It also summarises the relationship between the two methodologies: Six Sigma = TQM + customer focus + complementary data analysis tools + financial results + project management.

PRACTICAL APPLICATION

ADVICE AND TOP TIPS

We shall now apply the DMAIC methodology, outlined above, to practically visualise its contributions within a company. For a company to initiate a strategic transformation such as Six Sigma, it must effectively integrate the following five steps as a guideline.

- **Define the objective to reach for improvement.** This step allows you to guide the team so that all members go in the same direction. It also supports the analysis of the links between the different stages of the process and, therefore, the work on product improvement, identification of customer needs and the estimation of expected results. It is important to define the project objectively, quantifying it with a database. The data collection phase is a crucial step because it serves as a working basis for the entire project.
- **Measure the current production average.** It is vital to measure what the process is capable of producing and evaluate the number of defects. Thus, the Black Belts know the frequency of defects and make comparisons with the competition. It is important to focus on key elements of the process, meaning those with the biggest influence on quality. This step makes it possible to measure the sigma, the standard deviation of the process, which is useful to see the difference between the current average and the objective, the perfect average to reach.
- **Analyse further to identify what is causing the gap.**

The figures obtained are analysed in order to evaluate the performance of processes in relation to their ability and what competitors are doing. The purpose of this step is to calculate performance gaps (i.e. the differences between what is done today and what can be done in the future). We must therefore analyse the measurements obtained, look for root causes, validate them, etc.

- **Innovate to fill the standard deviation and move the average.** During this step, potential solutions must be proposed in order to plug loopholes present in the process and respond more to the performance expectations of customers.
- **Control new performance in terms of quality.** During this last stage, final checks must be made to maintain the level of quality achieved, and ensure an efficient and continuous development process. To do this, Black Belts implement certain actions to maintain the newly installed key elements in the workflow. They should also check that teams follow the process well, measure the results and validate the operation of the plan. If a new issue arises, Black Belts and their teams must be able to bounce back and rework the process immediately.

To summarise all of these steps, you must define the project, measure current performance, identify problems through analysis, innovate through relevant solutions and control the reconfigured process to ensure that the problem is truly solved.

According to the American economist George Eckes, to properly perform the strategic transformation of quality and effectively manage the process, it is useful to consider eight practical steps:

- collaboratively define an agreement of strategic objectives;
- create general processes, key sub-processes and implementation processes;
- appoint the Black Belts of the processes;
- establish a strategy in which the different teams define the steps and goals throughout the process;
- collect the necessary data for the chosen score-card;
- define the project selection criteria;
- select projects using these criteria;
- constantly manage the process to achieve the company's strategic goals.

CASE STUDY

The project of company X involves improving a decision-support tool (database) for the sellers, so that they can make forward sales estimates.

Project definition and project players

This project is implemented because many sellers are dissatisfied with this database, which is considered to be unreliable due to a lack of updates. The tool does not allow them to forecast sales correctly. Numerous interviews and studies are conducted to define the project, and also the main players:

- Priority is given to identifying the problem and the processes necessary to improve the decision-support tool. In our case, it involves finding a reliable way of predicting future financial stakes.
- A tool called 'stakeholder analysis' (taken from the EU training module on technical collaboration and advocacy) enables you to establish a template, positioning the different players and/or departments: finance department, sales department and IT department. The template shown by a grid organises the stakeholders according to their interests and power (low to high) and defines their attitude, influence and importance in terms of the objective.

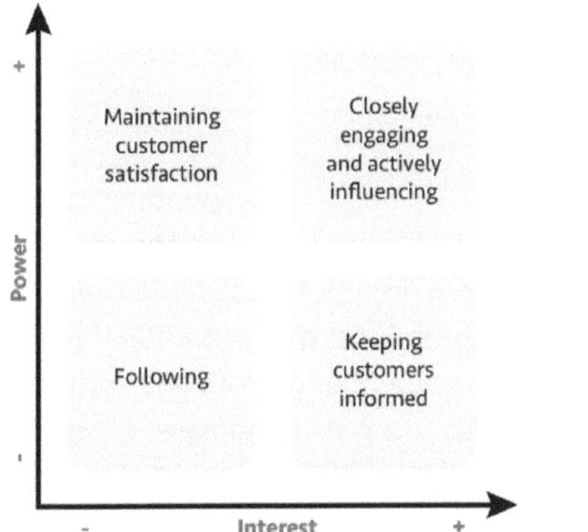

Moreover, for the project to be successfully carried out, the company must also convince some departments – including the IT department – who are reluctant and believe this to be an unnecessary step.

Measuring and analysing the ability of the process

Before you can define a new process, the team must take responsibility for the database and list the available information and steps, then investigate the potential added-value of the ideal tool. In other words, there needs to be an analysis according to products, product line, date of sale, etc., in order to identify gaps and improve data quality.

We must then find information internally (sales, inventory, product quality, etc.) which makes up a sufficiently representative part of the improvement process, to achieve a superior performance in terms of data quality. The team working on the project extracts 100 lots of data in order to analyse them and check with the sales teams which ones are undeniably reliable.

This determines a sample corresponding to a representative part of the total population of the country where the business is located, in order to observe the realities on the ground. Thus, for several days, the Black Belts work with sales teams to manually verify data and compare them with invoices. Findings are not immediate: among the invoices there may be some missing, duplicates or some that are incorrect.

The team is then responsible for determining the current performance and that to be achieved through new measures to implement via the Six Sigma system. Specifically, it aims for a correction of 1.5 sigma, transitioning from 4.5 to 6 sigma.

Performance following the misalignment of 1.5 sigma

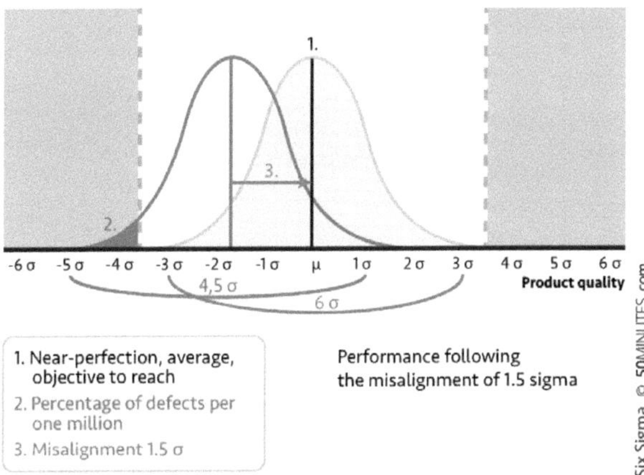

We can see that the transition from 4.5 to 6 sigma causes a significant drop in the defect rate, eventually reaching a reliability rate of 99.99% (i.e. the famous defect rate of 3.4 defects per million, expressed in volume below).

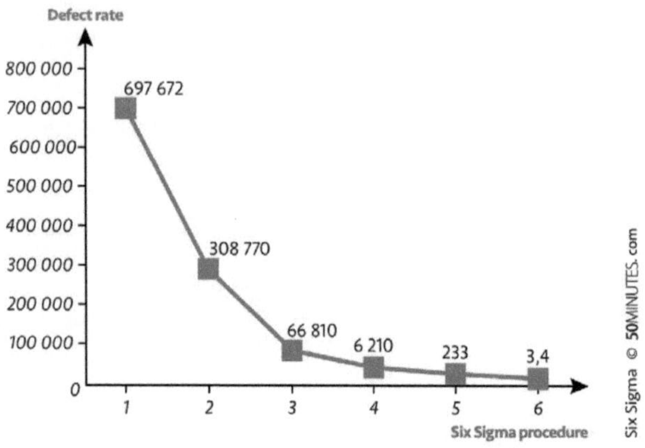

Changes in defect rate according to Six Sigma levels

After studying the data, experts identify the main defect that affects data quality, namely the improper handling of the tool by the sellers. This is due to a series of factors:

- too many people can encode information, but no responsibility is established;
- many observe a lack of interest and misinformed data.

The database, being relatively complex, suffers from shift changes and the imprecise use from people untrained in this kind of tool. They then measured the opportunities or sources of errors:

- incompetent people entering information;
- incorrect encoded data.

Recommendations

Here are the proposed solutions:

- establish access sessions to the database and identify the people who can benefit from them;
- make certain fields mandatory for those involved.

To apply these recommendations, a refocusing of the teams is required: only the team of sellers holds access to the database while the IT team is responsible for defining the required fields by users (sellers). The IT team then quickly implements the tools required while the sales team is more reticent. The manager of the IT team then provides an incentive scheme equivalent to a test (over a period of two months) that will identify the best seller (the one whose quality of encoded date is better) and reward him with a premium.

Monitoring the new process

Following this test, measures are taken to verify the reliability of this new method of data encoding. Among them, there are many statistical tools (such as the average and standard deviation). This last part, which is very important, is often overlooked due to lack of time, which undermines a number of initially well-executed projects.

SUMMARY

- Six Sigma is a statistical approach for businesses. It makes customers a central concern in order to attract them with improved product quality.
- There are three priorities: customers, employees and processes.
- For thirty years, companies such as Motorola, General Electric, Kodak and SFR have used Six Sigma to improve and gain or maintain a competitive advantage.
- When the Six Sigma objective is achieved, which in practice does not happen, there is an almost perfect reliability rating: 3.4 defects per one million defect opportunities (i.e. 99.99% reliability).
- The Six Sigma philosophy encourages a continuous reappraisal which is sustained over time (relentless pursuit of perfection).
- The whole company must participate for the implementation of the method to be successful.
- Six Sigma can fail if you only consider the technical aspects (cost reduction, etc.).
- If the change is not well managed in the company, possible results remain low.
- Lean Six Sigma is an extension of the method that focuses more on the production process.
- If you want to ensure the success of the approach, it is important to carefully follow the steps of the DMAIC methodology.

We want to hear from you!
Leave a comment on your online library
and share your favourite books on social media!

FURTHER READING

BIBLIOGRAPHY

- Ait Belkacem, E. H. (2005) *Puissance Six Sigma*. Paris: Dunod.
- Atmaca, E. and Gineres, S. S. (2013) Lean Six Sigma Methodology and Application. *Quality & Quantity*. 47(4).
- Berger, A. (2002) Six Sigma : un échelon en plus de la productivité ? *Dossier technique des pays de Savoie*.
- Eckes, G. (2001) *Objectif Six Sigma. La révolution dans la qualité*. Paris: Pearson.
- Kwak, Y. H. and Anbari, F. T. (2006) Benefits, Obstacles, and Future of Six Sigma Approach. *Technovation*. 6(5-6).
- Larson, A. (2003) *Demystifying Six Sigma: A company-Wide Approach to Continuous Improvement*. Amacon: American Management Association.
- Linderman, K., Schroeder, R. G., Zaher, S. and Choo, A. S. (2003) Six Sigma : a Goal-Theoretic Perspective. *Journal of Operation Management*. 21(2).
- Pande, P. S., Neuman, R. P., and Cavanagh, R. R. (2000) *The Six Sigma Way. How GE, MOTOROLA, and other top companies are honing their performance*. New-York: McGraw-Hill Companies.
- Truscott, W. T. (2003) *Six Sigma: Continual Improvement for Business*. Oxford: Butterworth Heinemann.